FAST CARS

Collector Card

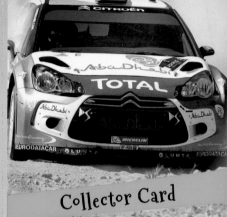

FAST CARS

Collector Card

FAST CARS

Collector Card

FAST CARS

Collector Card

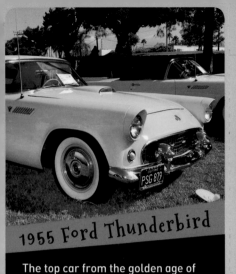

1955 Ford Thunderbird

The top car from the golden age of American cars.

	SCORE
RARITY FACTOR: 16,055 made	3
TOP SPEED: 193 km/h (120 mph)	5
PRICE: £1700	2
STYLE:	10

McLaren F1

Designed and built to be the 'ultimate road car'.

	SCORE
RARITY FACTOR: 106 made	6
TOP SPEED: 391 km/h (243 mph)	7
PRICE: £644,000	4
STYLE:	6

Thrust SSC

Thrust SSC can travel faster than the speed of sound.

	SCORE
RARITY FACTOR: 1 made	10
TOP SPEED: 1228 km/h (763 mph)	10
PRICE: £1.8 million	7
STYLE:	7

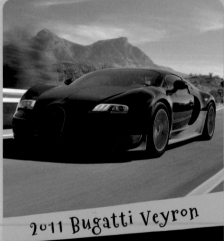

2011 Bugatti Veyron

One of the fastest cars that can be driven legally on public roads.

	SCORE
RARITY FACTOR: 40 made	7
TOP SPEED: 431 km/h (268 mph)	8
PRICE: £1.56 million	6
STYLE:	9

It's all about…

FAST
CARS

KINGFISHER

First published 2016 by Kingfisher
An imprint of Macmillan Children's Books
20 New Wharf Road, London N1 9RR
Associated companies throughout the world
www.panmacmillan.com

Series editor: Sarah Snashall
Series design: Anthony Hannant (LittleRedAnt)
Adapted from an original text by Chris Oxlade and Thea Feldman

ISBN 978-0-7534-3937-1

9 8 7 6 5 4 3 2 1

1TR/1115/WKT/UG/128MA

A CIP catalogue record for this book is available from the British Library.

Printed in China

Picture credits
The Publisher would like to thank the following for permission to reproduce their material.
Top = t; Bottom = b; Centre = c; Left = l; Right = r
Front cover, p1 Shutterstock/Rodrigo Garrido; Back cover Shutterstock/Richard Thornton;
Pages 2–3, 10–11, 30–31 Shutterstock/Max Earey; 4–5 Shutterstock/jiawangkun; 5t Getty/
Donaldon Collection; 5b Alamy/PC Jones; 6 Franz Haag; 7 Alamy/JELLE vanderwolf; 8–9 Alamy/
culture-images GmbH; 9t Alamy/Heritage Image Partnership Ltd; 9b Alamy/focusonmycar.com;
11t Alamy/Peter Wheeler; 11b Alamy/WENN Ltd; 12–13 Shutterstock/EvrenKalinBack;
13 Shutterstock/Action Sports Photography; 14 Shutterstock/Ahmad Faizal Yahya; 15t,
32 Shutterstock/David Acosta Allely; 15b Shutterstock/efcreata mediagroup;
16–17 Shutterstock/Alexander Kosarev; 17t Shutterstock/Christian Vinces; 18 Getty/David
Madison; 19 Getty/David Taylor; 20–21 Shutterstock/Peter Weber; 21 Shutterstock/Action
Sports Photography; 22–23 Alamy/Pictorial Press; 23t Getty/Handout; 23b Alamy/AF Archive;
24 Shutterstock/vladimir salman; 25 Corbis/Tim Wright; 26 Shutterstock/charnsitr; 27t NASA
27b Shutterstock/Mike Flippo; 28 AeroMobil; 29t Shutterstock/Joseph Sohm; 29b Alamy/
SiliconValleyStock.
Cards: Front tl Pat Durkin; tr McLaren; bl Getty/David Taylor; br Shutterstock/Max Earey;
Back tl Alamy/WENN Ltd; tr Shutterstock/luca85; bl Martin Durrschnabel; br NASA.

Front cover: A Citroen DS3 races in the 2013 Acropolis Rally of Greece.

CONTENTS

Cars all around

Cars come in many shapes and sizes. There are tiny cars and long cars. There are electric cars and bulletproof cars. And, of course, there are fast cars.

SPOTLIGHT: Ford Thunderbird

Manufacturer:	Ford Motor Company
Famous for:	first 'personal luxury car'
First built:	1955
Top speed:	193 km/h (120 mph)

FACT...

The American Dream is the longest car in the world. It is 30.5 metres long and has a helipad.

The tiny Peel Trident is just 183 centimetres long and 99 centimetres wide.

The first cars

Early cars looked a bit like horse-drawn carriages. They had big wheels and tiny engines, and they were very slow.

The Flocken Elektrowagen was the first electric car.

When cars were invented, most roads were rough tracks. There were no petrol stations, so drivers took cans of petrol with them in their car. Drivers also had to know how to mend their own car.

SPOTLIGHT: Benz Patent motor car

Manufacturer:	Karl Benz
Famous for:	first gasoline car
First built:	1885
Top speed:	16 km/h (10 mph)

FACT...

When the first cars started driving on the roads, a man with a red flag walked in front to warn slow-moving horse-drawn carriages.

Built for speed

Sports cars are built for speed. They have a smooth, rounded shape, a powerful engine and wide tyres that grip the road as they race around corners. Sports cars are exciting to drive, although they don't have room for lots of passengers and luggage.

The Lotus Elise can travel at speeds of up to 240 kilometres per hour (150 mph).

The Prince Henry
Austro-Daimler
was one of the first
sports cars.

The Mazda MX-5
is the bestselling
sports car in
the world.

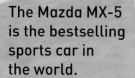

Supercars

Supercars are the fastest, rarest and most expensive sports cars. They have an incredibly powerful engine and a very lightweight body. Only a few of each model are made, and each car can cost over one million pounds.

Bugatti Veyron Supersport: top speed 431 km/h (268 mph)

FACT...

Supercars can drive at more than 400 kilometres per hour (248 mph). That's as fast as a speeding express train.

SPOTLIGHT: McLaren F1

Manufacturer:	McLaren Automotive
Famous for:	fastest production car in its day
First built:	1992
Top speed:	391 km/h (243 mph)

Hennessey Venom GT:
top speed 435 km/h (270 mph)

Track racers

You can see the thrills and spills of car racing at a race track. There are races for sports cars and for special racing cars. There are even races for family cars.

Road cars race around a track in Istanbul, Turkey.

The drivers sit inside a strong cage that protects them in case they crash. They wear a fireproof suit and a helmet.

FACT...

Racing drivers usually stop in the pits during a race to change the car's tyres. Their team can change all four tyres in just eight seconds.

All four tyres are usually changed at the same time during a pit stop.

Formula One

The fastest race cars are Formula One cars. They are specially built for track racing, with top-quality tyres and a low body to grip the surface of the track.

Formula One cars race in a series of races called Grand Prixes. At the end of the season there are two champions: one driver and one car constructor.

In a Formula One race, cars can reach speeds of 320 km/h (200 mph) or more.

Manufacturer:	Mercedes
Famous for:	Constructor Champion 2014
First built:	2014
Top speed:	estimated 300 km/h (186 mph)

Formula One driver Jenson Button prepares to race.

Rally racing

Rally races do not take place on a race circuit. Instead, the cars race from one point to another travelling along muddy roads and dirt tracks, choosing their own route. Sometimes they race through the snow and over frozen lakes.

Some rally races go
across the desert.

FACT...

In the Dakar Rally, the world's longest rally race,
cars can drive for up to 900 kilometres each day
across sand dunes, rocks, grass and mud.

The fastest car

The current land speed record is held by Thrust SSC, a jet-propelled, supersonic car. In 1997, fighter pilot Andy Green drove Thrust SSC at 1228 kilometres per hour (763 mph) in the desert in Nevada, USA.

New cars that might break the land speed record in the future are the Bloodhound SSC and the North American Eagle.

FACT...

Thrust SSC was the first land vehicle to travel faster than the speed of sound.

Thrust SSC travels faster than some jet planes.

Model name: Thrust SSC

Manufacturer: SSC Programme Limited
Famous for: holds world land speed record
First built: 1996
Top speed: 1228 km/h (763 mph)

Custom cars

Some car owners make their cars look weird and wonderful. They take off parts and add new ones, such as mirrors and wheels. Sometimes owners even change the actual shape of the car.

FACT...

Drag racers use parachutes to slow
down at the end of a race.

Some custom cars are built for
drag racing. These are called
dragsters. They race
each other along a
short track at
high speed.

Custom cars are often painted
with amazing patterns and
colourful pictures.

Movie cars

The most exciting cars sadly don't exist at all – except in films. James Bond's car, the Batmobile and Chitty Chitty Bang Bang all have impossible extra features. When writers create these cars they can let their imagination fly.

James Bond drives an Aston Martin equipped with rockets and an ejector seat.

FACT...

In the 2006 film *Cars*, all the characters are... cars!

The Batmobile has sophisticated weapons and special shields.

In the factory

Most cars are made in huge factories. Machines press and fold sheets of metal to make the car's body.

Robots do most of the work in a car-building factory.

FACT...

Car makers build more than 50 million new cars every year. That's one and a half cars every second!

The body moves through the factory. As it moves, the engine, the seats, the doors and all the other parts are fixed onto it. When the car is finished, it is tested to make sure all the parts work properly.

Cars containing crash-test dummies are crashed at high speed to check how safe they are.

Electric cars

Most of the 1000 million cars in the world run on petrol or diesel. They pollute the Earth's atmosphere.

Electric cars run off a huge battery. They are quiet and do not pollute the air, but they can't travel very far before they need to be recharged.

A hybrid car has both an engine and an electric motor. They use much less fuel than normal cars but are very expensive.

FACT...

The most expensive electric car of all time was only driven once and then abandoned – on the Moon!

It can take about eight hours to recharge an electric car.

Cars of the future

What kinds of car will we be driving in the future? Believe it or not, flying cars and driverless cars have already been developed. Flying cars have wings that can be tucked away. Driverless cars use cameras and sensors to drive.

Aeromobil's flying car has an autopilot and two parachutes.

The solar cells on this car use energy from sunlight to make electricity for the engine.

Google's driverless car uses a very detailed map to find its way around.

FACT...

It takes three minutes for Aeromobil's flying car to transform from a car into a plane.

29

GLOSSARY

atmosphere The layer of gases around the Earth (or around any planet).

constructor A person or company that builds something.

crash-test dummy A life-sized doll used to see what might happen to people in a car accident.

custom car A car that is one of a kind because it has been built to order or has been changed in some way.

diesel A type of fuel used in some cars.

engine The part of a car that makes it move.

fuel A liquid that burns inside an engine.

hybrid car A car that uses both electricity and fuel to run.

jet-propelled Something that is moved along by a jet engine.

land speed record The record for any vehicle travelling along the ground.

motor A machine that spins to provide movement. An electric motor changes electricity into movement energy.

parachute A large piece of cloth joined to thin ropes. It slows down dragster cars and people who are falling from a plane.

pits A special area at a race track where cars stop to have their wheels changed and fuel topped up.

pollution Waste that humans put into the environment. Gases from car engines are one kind of pollution.

production car A car that is mass produced in a factory for general use on the road.

rally A long-distance car race that often passes through places where it is difficult to drive.

recharge To refill a battery with electricity when the battery has run down.

INDEX

FAST CARS

Collector Card

FAST CARS

Collector Card

FAST CARS

Collector Card

FAST CARS

Collector Card

Hennessey Venom GT

This rarest supercar was test driven at the Kennedy Space Center, USA.

	SCORE
RARITY FACTOR: 3 made	8
TOP SPEED: 435 km/h (270 mph)	9
PRICE: £805,000	5
STYLE:	8

Lotus Elise

The 'affordable' sports car that is fun to drive.

	SCORE
RARITY FACTOR: 20,000+ made	2
TOP SPEED: 240 km/h (150 mph)	6
PRICE: £40,000	3
STYLE:	5

Benz Velocipede

The first car in the world to be produced in large numbers.

	SCORE
RARITY FACTOR: 1200 made	5
TOP SPEED: 20 km/h (13 mph)	2
PRICE: £750	1
STYLE:	2

Lunar Roving Vehicle

Current holder of the lunar land speed record!

	SCORE
RARITY FACTOR: 1 made	10
TOP SPEED: 18 km/h (11 mph)	1
PRICE: £24.5 million	10
STYLE:	1

Collect all the titles in this series!

BEASTLY
BUGS

FREE Collector Cards and Downloadable Audio!

DEADLY
DINOSAURS

FREE Collector Cards and Downloadable Audio!

FANTASTIC
FLIERS

FREE Collector Cards and Downloadable Audio!

FAST
CARS

FREE Collector Cards and Downloadable Audio!

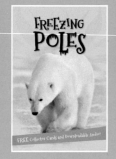

FREEZING
POLES

FREE Collector Cards and Downloadable Audio!

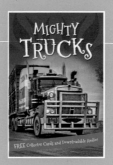

MIGHTY
TRUCKS

FREE Collector Cards and Downloadable Audio!

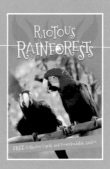

RIOTOUS
RAINFOREST

FREE Collector Cards and Downloadable Audio!

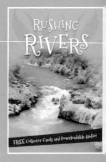

RUSHING
RIVERS

FREE Collector Cards and Downloadable Audio!